AF440331

WHEN YOU GROW, THEY GROW

Companion Workbook

The BRAVE Parent's Path from Reactive Fear to Convergent Living

80 pages • 14 modules • 12-week practice system

• Mirror Pair Diagnostic • Trigger Inventory • 21-Day BTR Log

• Story Archaeology • Identity Statement • Evidence Log

• Reflect Conversation Tracker • Mirror Pair Deep-Dives

• Stress Response Self-Assessment • Co-Parenting Scripts

• Progress Tracker • Mirror Journal (4 weeks)

• Letter to the Parent I Am Becoming

• Quick-Reference Hallway Cards • 12-Week Review

David Okonah

© Copyright DAO Publishing 2026

All rights reserved.

The content within this book may not be reproduced, duplicated or transmitted without direct written permission from the author or the publisher.

Under no circumstances will any blame or legal responsibility be held against the publisher or author for any damages, reparations, or monetary loss due to the information contained within this book. Either directly or indirectly. You are responsible for your own choices, actions, and results.

Legal Notice:

This book is copyright-protected. This book is only for personal use. You cannot amend, distribute, sell, use, quote, or paraphrase any part of this book's content without the author's or publisher's consent.

Disclaimer Notice:

Please note that the information contained within this document is for educational and entertainment purposes only. All effort has been expended to present accurate, up-to-date, reliable, and complete information. No warranties of any kind are declared or implied. Readers acknowledge that the author does not render legal, financial, medical, or professional advice. The content within this book has been derived from various sources. Please consult a licensed professional in your state before attempting any techniques outlined in this book.

By reading this document, the reader agrees that under no circumstances is the author responsible for any losses, direct or indirect, which are incurred as a result of the use of the information contained within this document, including, but not limited to, — errors, omissions, or inaccuracies.

All rights reserved.

First Edition

ISBN Numbers:

E book	**978-1-965551-15-8**
Paperback	**978-1-965551-16-5**
Hard copy	**978-1-965551-17-2**
Companion Workbook — Print Copy	**978-1-965551-18-9**
Companion Workbook — E book	**978-1-965551-26-4**

How to Use This Workbook

This workbook is your personal practice companion to *When You Grow, They Grow.* It is not a summary of the book. It is the space where the framework moves from understanding into action — where the three seconds where everything matters become three seconds you have practiced.

Each module corresponds directly to a core element of the BRAVE Framework or one of the five Mirror Pairs. You do not need to complete the workbook in sequence. Start with the module that is most alive for you right now.

Three ways to use this workbook

- **Alongside the book** — one module per chapter, as you read.
- **After the book** — returning to the practices that landed most.
- **With a co-parent** — sharing a module, comparing notes, and building a shared vocabulary.

The only standard for any entry in this workbook is honesty. Not the polished version. Not the version you would show a therapist. The version that is actually true when no one official is watching.

"The bravest thing a parent can do is let their child watch them become themselves."

Contents

Framework Quick Reference

Keep these pages in view as you work through the modules.

The BRAVE Framework

Five steps for the three seconds where every other approach has failed.

B

Breathe

One deliberate exhale. Interrupts the threat response before the reaction fires.

R

Recognize

Ask: What story am I telling myself right now?

A

Act

Ask: What would the parent I'm becoming do right now?

V

Voice

Make your growth visible to your child. One brief, honest sentence.

E

Evolve

Live the convergent life. Releasing and reclaiming as one continuous movement.

The Mirror Model

When you grow, your child grows — because you change the relational system you both live inside.

PAIR	WHEN THE PARENT...		THE CHILD...
01	**Trust** **Makes decisions without seeking validation**	→	Learns to trust their own judgment
02	**Boundaries** **Sets personal limits without guilt**	→	Learns that limits are safe
03	**Discomfort** **Sits with struggle without fixing it**	→	Develops genuine resilience
04	**Identity Beyond Role** **Pursues something that is theirs alone**	→	Gets permission to develop their own identity
05	**Courageous Visibility** **Takes visible risks in front of the child**	→	Inherits the model of a courageous adult life

BTR System: Breathe • Track • Reframe • Act • Reflect

The in-the-moment tool. Not on Sunday morning when you're calm — in the actual hallway, with the actual child, when it counts.

<table>
<tr><td>**00**</td><td>

Module 0 — Mirror Pair Diagnostic
Find your most active growth area

</td></tr>
</table>

Before anything else: find out which of the five Mirror Pairs is most active for you right now. This is not a test. There are no wrong answers. The most active pair is simply the one where the most growth is currently available.

How to Complete the Diagnostic

Read each statement. Score yourself from 1 (rarely true) to 5 (almost always true). Use your instinctive response — it is more accurate than a considered one.

Statement	1	2	3	4	5
I often seek external validation before making a parenting decision.	■	■	■	■	■
I find it hard to act on my own judgment without checking with someone first.	■	■	■	■	■
I feel anxious when I cannot confirm that my parenting choice was correct.	■	■	■	■	■
Mirror Pair 1 — TRUST score: ______ / 15					
I say "yes" when I mean "no" to avoid my child's displeasure.	■	■	■	■	■
I feel guilty when I set a limit for my own needs rather than my child's behavior.	■	■	■	■	■
I find it difficult to protect my own time, energy, or space without apologizing.	■	■	■	■	■
Mirror Pair 2 — BOUNDARIES score: ______ / 15					
I find it very difficult to watch my child struggle without intervening.	■	■	■	■	■

| I step in to fix problems my child could probably solve themselves. | ■ | ■ | ■ | ■ | ■ |
| My child's distress produces a physical urgency in me to act immediately. | ■ | ■ | ■ | ■ | ■ |

Mirror Pair 3 — DISCOMFORT TOLERANCE score: _______ / 15

I struggle to identify interests or pursuits that are mine and not related to parenting.	■	■	■	■	■
I feel guilty spending time on my own development rather than on my child's needs.	■	■	■	■	■
I am not sure who I am outside the parenting role.	■	■	■	■	■

Mirror Pair 4 — IDENTITY BEYOND ROLE score: _______ / 15

I keep my personal growth work private rather than making it visible to my child.	■	■	■	■	■
I avoid taking risks in front of my child because I am afraid of them seeing me fail.	■	■	■	■	■
I model caution and waiting rather than courage and trying.	■	■	■	■	■

Mirror Pair 5 — COURAGEOUS VISIBILITY score: _______ / 15

Reading Your Results

Your highest-scoring Mirror Pair is your most active pair right now. That is the pair where the most growth is available — and the pair whose module in this workbook will produce the most immediate impact.

| Trust: ___ | Boundaries: ___ | Discomfort: ___ |
| Identity: ___ | Courage: ___ | Most active pair: ___________ |

01   Module 1 — Trigger Inventory
Map your patterns before you practise

The BTR System works consistently when the triggers are named in advance. A trigger is not the situation — it is what the situation *means* to you. The same event elicits different reactions from different parents because the story beneath it differs.

Before completing the BTR Practice Log:

Work through this inventory first. Name your three most recurring triggers, the stories beneath them, and the discomfort they are actually managing. The Log then becomes training for known territory rather than surprised documentation.

Stress Response Self-Assessment (NEW)

Before mapping triggers, identify your autonomic tendency — which state your nervous system defaults to under pressure.

When triggered, I notice:	Likely state	Me? ■
I tend to raise my voice or escalate quickly	Fight / Flight	
I go quiet and withdraw when triggered	Freeze / Fawn	
I feel a physical urgency to fix or act immediately	Flight / Fawn	
I feel my heart rate increase before I have a conscious thought	Fight / Flight	
I apologise or placate even when I am right	Fawn	

I freeze and feel unable to respond at all	Freeze	

My primary stress response pattern:

Where in my body does the trigger land first (before my mind registers it):

Exercise 1.1 — Your Trigger Inventory

List three recent parenting moments where you reacted in a way you would not have chosen.

Trigger Moment 1

What happened (the situation, briefly):

What I did (the reactive response):

The story I was telling myself (Track step):

Whose discomfort was I managing — mine or theirs?

What the parent I'm becoming would have done instead (Act step):

Trigger Moment 2

What happened (the situation, briefly):

What I did (the reactive response):

The story I was telling myself (Track step):

Whose discomfort was I managing — mine or theirs?

What the parent I'm becoming would have done instead (Act step):

Trigger Moment 3

What happened (the situation, briefly):

What I did (the reactive response):

The story I was telling myself (Track step):

Whose discomfort was I managing — mine or theirs?

What the parent I'm becoming would have done instead (Act step):

Patterns I notice looking across the three moments:

02   Module 2 — The BRAVE Framework: (B)reathe
The exhale as circuitry

"The single exhale is not breathing as relaxation. It is breathing as an interruption. As circuitry. As the three-second gap where your entire future as a parent becomes possible."

The Breathe step works because it stimulates the vagal brake — the physiological mechanism that interrupts the threat response at its neurological source. It requires no equipment, no training, and no perfect conditions. It requires one exhale.

Breathe Practice Menu

Match your practice technique to your stress response pattern identified in Module 1.

If your pattern is Fight/Flight	If your pattern is Freeze/Fawn
4-count exhale: breathe in 4, out for 8. The extended exhale activates the vagal brake directly.	Sighing exhale: one audible sigh through the mouth. Releases the held tension of the freeze state.
Box breathing (high-load moments)	**Grounding exhale (dissociated moments)**
In 4, hold 4, out 4, hold 4. Regulates the nervous system through rhythmic pattern.	Breathe in through nose, exhale slowly while pressing feet into the floor. Reorients to present.

The Eight Low-Stakes Practice Scenarios

- The incoming text — before you open it, one exhale.
- The front door — before you open it, one exhale.
- The homework question — before you answer, one exhale.
- The dinner table silence — before you speak, one exhale.

- The announcement — before you respond, one exhale.
- The overheard conversation — before you act, one exhale.
- The apology window — before you go to repair, one exhale.
- The no-trigger moment — once daily, for no reason at all.

Exercise 2.1 — 21-Day Breathe Log (NEW: 3 Weeks)

The Breathe muscle is built across weeks, not days. Complete three consecutive seven-day blocks. The gaps between blocks are as instructive as the entries.

Week 1

Day	Situation	Gap?	Note
Monday		■ Y ■ N	
Tuesday		■ Y ■ N	
Wednesday		■ Y ■ N	
Thursday		■ Y ■ N	
Friday		■ Y ■ N	
Saturday		■ Y ■ N	
Sunday		■ Y ■ N	

End of Week 1 reflection — what I noticed:

Week 2

Day	Situation	Gap?	Note
Monday		■ Y ■ N	
Tuesday		■ Y ■ N	

Day	Situation	Gap?	Note
Wednesday		■ Y ■ N	
Thursday		■ Y ■ N	
Friday		■ Y ■ N	
Saturday		■ Y ■ N	
Sunday		■ Y ■ N	

End of Week 2 reflection — what I noticed:

Week 3

Day	Situation	Gap?	Note
Monday		■ Y ■ N	
Tuesday		■ Y ■ N	
Wednesday		■ Y ■ N	
Thursday		■ Y ■ N	
Friday		■ Y ■ N	
Saturday		■ Y ■ N	
Sunday		■ Y ■ N	

End of Week 3 reflection — what I noticed:

<table>
<tr><td>**03**</td><td># Module 3 — The BRAVE Framework: (R)ecognize
Separate trigger from story</td></tr>
</table>

The Track question — *What story am I telling myself?* — creates the gap in which the reactive response becomes a chosen response. But it has one common obstacle: the story that has been running so long it feels like a fact.

"Is this story mine — or is this story data?"

Exercise 3.1 — Story Archaeology

Identify one story you tell yourself repeatedly in relation to your child or the parenting transition.

The story (in your own words — the exact way you tell it to yourself):

How long have I been telling this story?

What evidence supports this story? (What I have actually observed, not interpreted)

What evidence contradicts this story? (Moments that do not fit the narrative)

What would the data say if the story were stripped away?

What response does the story produce — and is that the response I want to be giving?

Exercise 3.2 — The Recognize Practice Log

For the next two weeks, use this log after any significant trigger moment to complete the Recognize step. The goal is not to analyze the trigger in depth — it is to practise the habit of quickly asking the Track question.

Entry 1

Date / Situation:

Story I told myself (Track):

Story or data? (Reframe):

Identity-aligned response (Act):

Entry 2

Date / Situation:

Story I told myself (Track):

Exercise 3.2 — The Recognize Practice Log

Story or data? (Reframe):

Identity-aligned response (Act):

Entry 3

Date / Situation:

Story I told myself (Track):

Story or data? (Reframe):

Identity-aligned response (Act):

Entry 4

Date / Situation:

Story I told myself (Track):

Story or data? (Reframe):

Identity-aligned response (Act):

<table>
<tr><td>**04**</td><td>## Module 4 — The BRAVE Framework: (A)ct
Build the identity that acts differently</td></tr>
</table>

The Identity Question — *What would the parent I'm becoming do right now?* — is the Act step's core tool. It works not by overriding the reactive response but by providing the nervous system with a pre-loaded identity pattern to access instead.

Exercise 4.1 — Building Your Identity Statement

Before the Identity Question can be answered quickly under pressure, the identity it refers to needs to be specific enough to be recognisable. Complete the exercise below.

In three words, the parent I'm becoming is:

The parent I'm becoming responds to difficulty by:

The parent I'm becoming trusts:

The parent I'm becoming is visibly different from the parent I have been in these ways:

The parent I'm becoming is not yet:

My Identity Statement:

The parent I am becoming ________________________________,
and when I encounter difficulty I respond by
________________________________. I trust my own judgment to
________________________________.

Exercise 4.2 — The Evidence Log

After each identity-aligned response — however small, however imperfect — complete one entry below. Evidence is the currency of identity change. The parent who can point to ten moments of acting differently has proof.

#	Date / Situation	What I did differently	What happened next
1			
2			
3			
4			
5			
6			
7			
8			
9			
10			

<table><tr><td>**05**</td><td># Module 5 — The BRAVE Framework: (V)oice
Make your becoming visible</td></tr></table>

The Reflect conversation is the Voice step made real. It is a brief, honest exchange in which you make your becoming visible to your child. It does not require a response. It requires only that it is genuine.

"It's not the calm response that teaches your child the most. It's the visible effort to achieve it."

Exercise 5.1 — Writing Your Reflect Conversations

After a reactive response you couldn't catch:

My version:

Reminder: Brief. Honest. No request for forgiveness. No explanation of the framework.

After a moment that went better than expected:

My version:

Reminder: Name the choice — not just the outcome. 'I noticed I paused...' not 'I'm glad that went well.'

When you're not sure what to say:

My version:

Reminder: Your seven-word version: 'I'm working on something. You might have noticed.' — or your own version.

Exercise 5.2 — Reflect Conversation Tracker

Record each Reflect conversation you have across the next four weeks.

Reflect Conversation 1

Date / Context:

What I said (as close to verbatim as possible):

How it was received:

What I observed in the days that followed:

Reflect Conversation 2

Date / Context:

What I said (as close to verbatim as possible):

How it was received:

What I observed in the days that followed:

Reflect Conversation 3

Date / Context:

What I said (as close to verbatim as possible):

How it was received:

What I observed in the days that followed:

Reflect Conversation 4

Date / Context:

What I said (as close to verbatim as possible):

How it was received:

What I observed in the days that followed:

Reflect Conversation 5

Date / Context:

What I said (as close to verbatim as possible):

How it was received:

What I observed in the days that followed:

Reflect Conversation 6

Date / Context:

What I said (as close to verbatim as possible):

How it was received:

What I observed in the days that followed:

06 — Module 6 — The BRAVE Framework: (E)volve
Design the convergent life

The Evolve step is the BRAVE Framework integrated — the point at which the five steps become not a tool to deploy but a way of being. It is also where the convergent life is designed.

Exercise 6.1 — The Three Convergent Life Questions

Take the time this deserves. Not the five-minute version — the thirty-minute version. Write more than you think you need to.

Question 1	*What does my Tuesday look like when I'm fully alive? Not the fantasy Tuesday. The realistic, attainable, this-could-actually-be-my-life Tuesday. What's in it? What's mine in it?*

Question 2	*What does my relationship with my child look like when it's built on mutual respect rather than obligation? What does it feel like? What do we talk about? What does the voluntary phone call sound like?*

Question 3	*What is the one door I've been standing in front of for years that the convergent life requires me to open? Not someday. This year. This month. What is it?*

In one sentence, the door I am going to open:

The first small step I can take this week is:

The person I will tell about it is:

07 Module 7 — Mirror Pair 1: Trust
Deep-dive practice

The parent who cannot trust themselves raises a child who cannot trust themselves — and neither of them knows that is what is happening.

Trust	When the parent...	The child...
	Makes one parenting decision per day without seeking external validation	Develops an internal locus of control — trusts their own judgment

The Four-Week Trust Practice

Week	Focus	My notes / observations
Week 1	Identify every moment I seek validation before acting. Do not change it yet — just see it.	
Week 2	Delay the validation-seeking by two hours. Decide first, consult later if still needed.	
Week 3	Make one decision per day without consulting at all. Note the discomfort and the outcome.	
Week 4	Review Week 3 decisions. How often did I need the validation I did not seek?	

The three most significant decisions I made on my own judgment this month:

What I noticed about my child's behavior when I stopped seeking validation:

Mirror Pair 1 — Observation: What have I noticed in my child this month that I did not manage, direct, or organise?

08   Module 8 — Mirror Pair 2: Boundaries
Deep-dive practice

The Boundaries practice is not about setting limits for your child. It is about setting limits for your own life — and letting your child watch you do it.

Boundaries	When the parent...	The child...
	Sets personal limits without guilt or apology	Learns that limits are self-respecting, not rejecting

Exercise 8.1 — Boundary Language Practice

The language of a genuine boundary is stated in the first person, requires no justification, and does not request permission. Rewrite each reactive default as an identity-aligned boundary.

> **Reactive:** *I hope you don't mind, but I was thinking I might need this evening to myself...?*
>
> Identity-aligned:

> **Reactive:** *I'll sort it this time, but you really do need to start taking responsibility...*
>
> Identity-aligned:

Reactive: Write your own reactive default that you most often use:

My identity-aligned version:

The specific boundary I have been unwilling to set:

What I have been telling myself about why I cannot set it:

The identity-aligned version — what I will say when I set it:

When I will set it:

Mirror Pair 2 — Observation: What have I noticed in my child this month that I did not manage, direct, or organise?

09   Module 9 — Mirror Pair 3: Discomfort Tolerance
Deep-dive practice

Every rescue operation a parent runs is funded by love — and every one of them quietly confirms to the child that they cannot survive without it.

Discomfort Tolerance	When the parent...	The child...
	Asks 'What's your next step?' instead of providing the next step	Develops genuine resilience through the experience of coping

Exercise 9.1 — The Rescue Audit

Three situations where I regularly intervene in my child's difficulty:

In each case, whose discomfort am I primarily managing — mine or theirs?

The physical sensation I feel when I resist the rescue impulse:

The story I tell myself about why my child needs me to intervene:

The Three-Second Pause — Practice Levels

- **Level 1:** Pause before intervening. Ask "Whose discomfort?" Then intervene if genuinely needed. The pause is the practice.
- **Level 2:** Pause. Ask the question. Wait 30 seconds. Often the child solves it themselves.
- **Level 3:** Pause. Say: "I can see this is hard. What's your next step?" Then wait.

The level I am consistently at right now:

The level I am working toward:

The specific situation where I most need to move to Level 3:

Mirror Pair 3 — Observation: What have I noticed in my child this month that I did not manage, direct, or organise?

10　Module 10 — Mirror Pair 4: Identity Beyond Role
Deep-dive practice

You were someone before you became a parent. That person did not die. They went quiet. This practice is not reinvention. It is an excavation.

Identity Beyond Role	When the parent...	The child...
	Pursues one weekly practice that is theirs alone, visibly and without apology	Receives permission to develop their own separate identity

Exercise 10.1 — The Identity Archaeology

Before parenthood consumed the majority of my time and identity, what did I love doing?

If the guilt were absent for one week — if no one would judge me — what would I do?

What have I been saying 'maybe someday' about for the longest?

Who is the version of myself I occasionally catch a glimpse of in a rare unscheduled hour?

> **If the Archaeology Produces Nothing — Four Entry Points:**
>
> - **The Absorption Test:** What activity makes time pass without my noticing?
>
> - **The Envy Map:** What do I feel hungry for when I hear someone describe their life?
>
> - **The Pre-Performance Self:** What did I do before it became something I did for others?
>
> - **The One-Hour Experiment:** Try one thing for one hour with no expectation of it being the right thing.

The weekly practice I am committing to (specific, visible, without apology):

When in the week it happens:

How I will make it visible to my child:

> **Mirror Pair 4 — Observation: What have I noticed in my child this month that I did not manage, direct, or organise?**

<table>
<tr><td>11</td><td>

Module 11 — Mirror Pair 5: Courageous Visibility
Deep-dive practice
</td></tr>
</table>

Your child is not learning from your words about courage. They are learning from watching you practise it.

Courageous Visibility	When the parent...	The child...
	Takes one visible act of personal courage per month in the child's presence	Inherits the model of a courageous adult life

Exercise 11.1 — The Courage Inventory

What have I been postponing because of what people might think?

What would I do if I knew my child would see it as brave rather than embarrassing?

What has been 'not the right time' for so long that the timing has become the excuse?

What did I stop doing when the parenting role consumed everything?

What would be the most visible possible expression of who I am becoming?

The Monthly Courage Practice

One visible act of personal courage per month. Done openly. Not hidden, not minimised when the family notices.

Month	The courage act	What my child witnessed / what I noticed
Month 1		
Month 2		
Month 3		

Month	The courage act	What my child witnessed / what I noticed
Month 4		
Month 5		
Month 6		

Mirror Pair 5 — Observation: What have I noticed in my child this month that I did not manage, direct, or organise?

Midpoint Check-In — Week 6

Pause here. Before continuing to the Mirror Journal and the final modules, use these prompts to assess your progress at the halfway mark.

What has been the most surprising shift in my parenting since beginning this work?

Which BTR step do I reach for most naturally now? Which step is still hard?

What has my child done in the last six weeks that I did not manage, direct, or organise?

What part of the framework have I been avoiding — and what might that avoidance be protecting?

The one word that describes who I am becoming, that I could not have used six weeks ago:

12　Module 12 — The Mirror Journal
4-week evidence record

The Mirror Journal is your ongoing practice log. It is not a diary. It is an evidence record — the place where the BRAVE work becomes visible across weeks and months. Use one page per week. The questions are the same each week — consistency is the point. Reading back across four weeks produces something that is invisible in any single entry.

> *"The knowing-doing gap closes not when the parent learns more. It closes when the parent practises enough that the doing becomes as automatic as the knowing has always been."*

Week 1 — Mirror Journal Entry

Date: ______________

The reactive moment this week (if any):

What I did differently this week:

The BTR step I used most:

My most active Mirror Pair this week:

What I noticed in my child:

The door I am still standing in front of:

One sentence I said out loud that I would not have said three months ago:

My stress response pattern this week — how it showed up:

Week 2 — Mirror Journal Entry

Date: _______________

The reactive moment this week (if any):

What I did differently this week:

The BTR step I used most:

My most active Mirror Pair this week:

What I noticed in my child:

The door I am still standing in front of:

One sentence I said out loud that I would not have said three months ago:

My stress response pattern this week — how it showed up:

Week 3 — Mirror Journal Entry

Date:
____

The reactive moment this week (if any):

What I did differently this week:

The BTR step I used most:

My most active Mirror Pair this week:

What I noticed in my child:

The door I am still standing in front of:

One sentence I said out loud that I would not have said three months ago:

My stress response pattern this week — how it showed up:

Week 4 — Mirror Journal Entry

Date: ___________

The reactive moment this week (if any):

What I did differently this week:

The BTR step I used most:

My most active Mirror Pair this week:

What I noticed in my child:

The door I am still standing in front of:

One sentence I said out loud that I would not have said three months ago:

My stress response pattern this week — how it showed up:

12   Module 12 — Extended Mirror Journal
Weeks 5–8: Deepening the pattern

Weeks 5–8 shift the focus from observing patterns to interpreting them. The prompts for Week 5 onward include two new questions: one about the pattern itself, and one that turns toward the future.

Week 5 — Mirror Journal Entry

Date:
____

The reactive moment this week (if any):

What I did differently this week:

The BTR step I used most:

My most active Mirror Pair this week:

What I noticed in my child:

What the pattern across my last four weeks tells me:

The door I am still standing in front of:

One sentence I said out loud that I would not have said at Week 1:

Week 6 — Mirror Journal Entry

Date: _______________

The reactive moment this week (if any):

What I did differently this week:

The BTR step I used most:

My most active Mirror Pair this week:

What I noticed in my child:

What the pattern across my last four weeks tells me:

The door I am still standing in front of:

One sentence I said out loud that I would not have said at Week 1:

Week 7 — Mirror Journal Entry

Date: ___________

The reactive moment this week (if any):

What I did differently this week:

The BTR step I used most:

My most active Mirror Pair this week:

What I noticed in my child:

What the pattern across my last four weeks tells me:

The door I am still standing in front of:

One sentence I said out loud that I would not have said at Week 1:

Week 8 — Mirror Journal Entry

Date: ______________

The reactive moment this week (if any):

What I did differently this week:

The BTR step I used most:

My most active Mirror Pair this week:

What I noticed in my child:

What the pattern across my last four weeks tells me:

The door I am still standing in front of:

One sentence I said out loud that I would not have said at Week 1:

13 Module 13 — The Co-Parenting Dimension
Shared vocabulary, shared direction

This module is designed to be completed individually first — and then, if both partners are willing, shared. The goal is a shared vocabulary and a shared direction. Not a hierarchy. Not one partner ahead of the other.

Individual Reflection — Complete Before Sharing

My most active Mirror Pair right now (from Module 0):

The Mirror Pair I observe as most active in my co-parent:

The way our Mirror Pair patterns interact — where they amplify each other, where they create friction:

The one thing I want my co-parent to understand about where I am in this work:

The one thing I am willing to ask of my co-parent as I do this work:

Shared Conversation Prompts

If your co-parent is willing to engage with this module, use these prompts as starting points. Not as a diagnostic session. As a conversation between two people navigating the same transition from different positions.

Which of the five Mirror Pairs feels most active for you right now?

What did you set aside when the parenting role consumed everything?

What would the next chapter of your life look like if you gave it permission?

What do you want our child to have witnessed in us by the time they are thirty?

Co-Parenting Script Builder (NEW)

Use these templates to prepare for specific conversations — before the moment arrives.

The Resistant Co-Parent Conversation

What I want to say: use Voice step structure — brief, honest, no demand for immediate alignment.

My script:

The Separated Parent Handover Moment

What I can control in this moment: the exhale, the one sentence, the response I choose.

My script:

Asking My Honest Witness for Support

What I need from this person: specific, observable, time-bound.

My script:

For the Parent Doing This Alone

If you are reading this module without a co-parenting partner — by choice, by circumstance, or by loss — this section is yours.

The one person in my life who can serve as my honest witness for this work:

What I will ask of them:

The date I will have that conversation:

00   Progress Tracker
Weekly at-a-glance evidence of movement

Use this tracker alongside the Mirror Journal. The three columns work together: the active BRAVE step tells you where your practice is focused; the Mirror Pair shows whether your most active pair is shifting; the Evidence Log tally shows accumulated proof of change.

Week	Most active BRAVE step	Most active Mirror Pair	Evidence entries (total)
Week 1			
Week 2			
Week 3			
Week 4			
Week 5			
Week 6			
Week 7			
Week 8			
Week 9			
Week 10			
Week 11			

Week	Most active BRAVE step	Most active Mirror Pair	Evidence entries (total)
Week 12			

Mirror Pair at Week 1 (from Diagnostic):

Mirror Pair at Week 12 (re-take Diagnostic):

Letter to the Parent I Am Becoming

Instructions: Write this letter at the beginning of Week 1. Write honestly, without editing. Seal it — physically fold this page inward — and do not read it again until the 12-Week Review.

Write to the parent you intend to become. Not the ideal version — the honest, specific, reachable version. What do you want to have changed? What do you want your child to have witnessed? What door will you have opened?

Date written: ________________ *Open on:* ________________

Dear ________________,

____

____

____

____

____

____

____

____

____

____

____

From, the parent I am right now. ______________

(continue on this page if needed)

Quick-Reference Hallway Cards

Keep these in view — on your phone, on the fridge, or anywhere accessible in the moment. Each card is the complete tool in its shortest form.

THE BRAVE FRAMEWORK — In the hallway, right now

- B — One exhale. Before the reaction fires.

- R — "What story am I telling myself right now?"

- A — "What would the parent I'm becoming do?"

- V — One brief honest sentence. No explanation.

- E — The releasing and the reclaiming are one movement.

THE BTR SYSTEM — When the trigger fires

- Breathe — One deliberate exhale first. Always.

- Track — "What story is running?"

- Reframe — "Story or data?"

- Act — The identity-aligned response. Now.

- Reflect — One honest sentence afterward.

MY MIRROR PAIR THIS WEEK

• My most active pair right now: ___________________

• The parent practice I am working on: ___________________

• What my child is learning from this: ___________________

• One thing I will do differently today: ___________________

14 Module 14 — The 12-Week Review
Read back. See what changed.

Before you answer these questions:

Read back through every entry in your Mirror Journal. Read back through your Evidence Log. If you wrote the Letter to the Parent I Am Becoming in the previous section — open it now and read it first. Take your time. The review is the evidence.

"The knowing-doing gap closes not with a single moment of insight.
It closes with forty-seven ordinary moments, accumulated quietly,
until the system around you shifts because you have."

The Evidence Review

The three most significant identity-aligned responses I made in the last twelve weeks:

The reactive patterns that have been reduced or changed:

What I have noticed in my child that I attribute to my own growth (not their management):

The Mirror Pair I entered this work in. The Mirror Pair I am at now:

The door I said I would open. What happened:

The Convergent Life Assessment

Return to the three convergent life questions from Module 6. Read what you wrote twelve weeks ago. Then answer this:

What has changed between the parent who wrote those answers and the parent writing this?

What has not changed — and what that tells me about where the next twelve weeks of work live:

The voluntary phone call. Is it coming? Is it already here? What does it sound like?

The most important sentence I can write right now, about who I am becoming:

The work is not finished because the workbook is.

The workbook is finished because you are ready to live it.

When you grow, they grow.

This has always been true. These pages show you how to live it.

David Okonah
When You Grow, They Grow • The BRAVE Parent's Path
Professional Series editions — Facilitator Guide and Pro Series Companion Workbook — available separately.

www.ingramcontent.com/pod-product-compliance
Lightning Source LLC
Chambersburg PA
CBHW061430050726
47593CB00006B/2298